John Hegley

FIVE
SUGARS
PLEASE

with drawings by the author

Methuen

Also by John Hegley

Glad to Wear Glasses
Can I Come Down Now
These Were Your Father'
Love Cuts
The Family Pack
Beyond Our Kennel
Dog

Saint and Blurry (Rykodi

Published by Methuen 2001

10 9 8 7 6 5 4 3 2 1

First published in Great Britain in 1993 by Methuen London

First published in paperback in Great Britain in 1994 by Mandarin Paperbacks

This edition, with a new cover design, published in the United Kingdom in 2001 by
Methuen Publishing Limited
215 Vauxhall Bridge Road, London SW1V 1EJ

Methuen Publishing Limited Reg. No. 3543167

A CIP catalogue record for this book is available from the British Library

ISBN 0 413 77300 0

Printed and bound in Great Britain by
Cox and Wyman Ltd, Reading, Berkshire

Five Sug

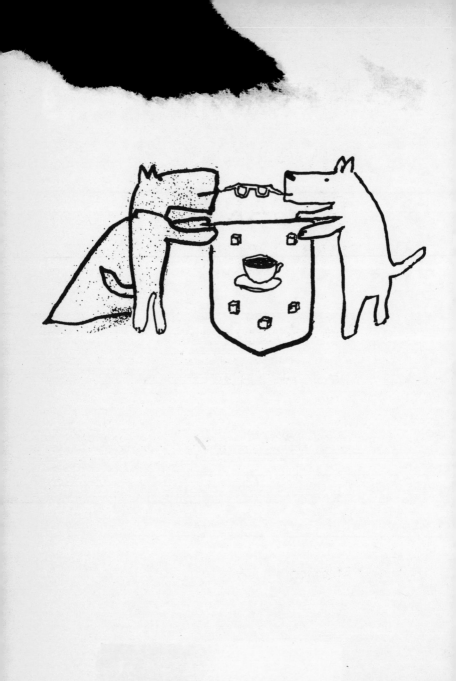

Contents

On the boards in the glasses 9
A Christmas cabaret 10
Glasses good, contact lenses bad 11
Christmas poetry 12
Give me five 13
The old Roman cafe 14
Cafe closed 16
The love between two dogs 17
Rex 18
Leaving the festival 19
Guy 20
Bonfire feelings 21
Pat at the pool table 22
Malcolm 23
The PhanTom 24
The trouble with the tampao 25
The manœuvre 26
Popping out for a paper 27
McKenna 28
Overwriting the Bank of England 31
Spring 32
Summer 33
Italian holiday snap 33
Autumn 34
Sumo 35
Snakes and sheds 36
Street poets 37
A Martian tries to buy a drink 38
A fisher of words 39
A poem with a pong 39
A Bradford curry house 40
Relaxing with taxidermy 41
Masher 42
A spelling of spuds 43
The difference between truth and adequacy 44

The difference between dogs and sheds 45
A short address at the comedy college 46
Old pals 47
Allez 48
French letters – English words 49
The common poetry 50
Easter Eggley 52
Cause to quibble 53
His poems are his children 54
Children's show time-to-go poem 55
John put upon 56
Colette upset 57
The parade of not-forgetting 58
The Christmas bonus 60
Neck 61
Top of the choppers 62
Grandma's footsteps 63
The gift 64
Borderline decision 65
The crest of a waving 66
The Cumbrian cutting 68
Not my cup of coffee 69
Tales from the tent 70
Friendship in the Mendip Hills 71
The creeping sleeping bag 72
The power of rhyme 73
Talking about my feelings ain't my cup of tea 74
J for jealous 76
Meditation on 'The Raising of the Cross' by Rembrandt 78
Outsider art 79
Otto Dix art attack 80
My brother's advice 81
My father's admonishment 82

Greed   83
The daily bread   84
Poem without a heart   85
Trains in India   86
Fresh in Edinburgh   86
The flannel   87
Declaring Martian Law   89

On the boards in the glasses

The first time I walked on stage
someone called out 'hey
look it's Buddy Holly!'
It's not what you'd expect in a nativity play.

A Christmas cabaret

It was the opening occasion
of the New Messiah Club,
they were gathered round the manger
in a room behind a pub.
Hosting on that evening
was a man who worked with wood
and his wife who did the magic
who was also very good.
She introduced a brand new act
they all seemed to adore
and all he did was lie there
on a little bed of straw.
Then the one who brought the frankincense
upset the one who brought the sheep.
'If you don't like the smell in here,' he said,
'you know what you can do, you creep.'
'Shut it boys, I'm trying to sleep,'
cut in the baby on the straw,
'and if you think the fact that I can speak's a miracle
just wait until my encore.'

Glasses good, contact lenses bad

In the embrace of my glasses
I openly accept my vulnerability
and affirm my acceptance of outside help.
As well as providing open acknowledgment
of the imperfection in my eyesight
my glasses are a symbolic celebration
of the wider imperfection that is the human condition.
In contrast contact lenses are a hiding of the fault
they pretend the self-sufficiency of the individual
and minister unto the cult of stultifying normality,
they are that which should be cast out of your vision:
they are a denial of the self,
they are a denial of the other,
they are a betrayal of humanity.

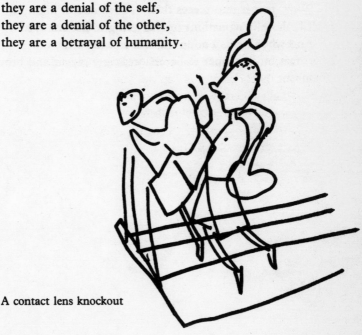

A contact lens knockout

Christmas poetry

One Christmas my father gave me and my sister a sheet of brown paper each for our main present and said that this year we could enjoy the greatest gift of all – the imagination.

'Children,' he said cheerily, 'these are your magic carpets.'

'But dad,' I complained, 'I wanted a sheet of brown paper.'

'And I wanted a wrapped up present,' complained my sister.

'But this present is its own wrapping paper,' said our father, confusing her rather.

'But she wanted a jigsaw, dad,' I added.

'Well, tear it into pieces then,' added dad in his turn. 'USE those imaginations or I'm going to get annoyed!'

And when he had gone we each imagined the other person's brown paper to be unacceptably bigger and browner than our own.

Give me five

This dog walks into a South London greasy spoon dressed like a Roman centurion.

'A large tea please, when you're ready,' he says to the proprietor. And the proprietor says 'sugar?'

The old Roman cafe

'A weak tea please,' said John to the man in the white jacket.

'Sugar?' said the man.

Inspired by the establishment's title, John imagined making a 'V' sign and then saying 'Yes, I'll have five – five sugars please.' Not to cause confrontation but to make a quick camaraderie in the way that dogs do.

But the man probably had his mind more in the present mode and might not have seen the joke and even if he had he might have thought it was useless and he might not want to behave like a dog.

John didn't take sugar anyway.

As he was sipping his cuppa it occurred to him that sugar might well have been unknown in ancient Rome. It came from deep down in Africa, didn't it – way beyond the stretch of the Empire's fingers?

John gestured that he would like to speak to the white-jacketed gentleman.

'Changed your mind about the sugar?'

'No . . .'

'It's all right if you have, you know. No problem, as they say on the continent.'

'I was just wondering, do you think they took sugar in their tea in ancient Rome?'

'I don't know if they had tea in Roman times, Sir.'

'Mm but they might have had other beverages and taken sugar in those.'

'If they had sugar, that is.'

'That's what I mean, that's what I want to know, Mister . . . ?'

'Harry . . . Call me Harry, everybody else does. It's my

name you see, sir,' Harry said playfully, and John thought it
was a great little joke and wondered if he'd heard it
anywhere before. If he hadn't, he wondered if it would be
immoral to use it in his work. It wouldn't harm Harry in any
way: their respective publics would almost certainly never
coincide . . .

'You seem very thoughtful, sir.'

'Oh . . . I was just wondering . . .'

'Wondering about sugar?'

'No – I was wondering whether you'd mind me using that
line about your name and people calling you it because that's
what it is.'

'You're losing me now sir.'

'I know I am, I'm sorry.'

'I'm not sure about the Romans, I'm afraid; I've never
been much of a scholar. I think perhaps the local public
lending library might be able to help . . .'

'I'm sorry I've alienated you, Harry. Forgive me. You
opened yourself to me and I just went straight back into my
own world at the first opportunity . . .'

'Cup or mug, sir?'

'A mug, definitely.'

Cafe closed

They'd seen over half a century turn
earning from their English urn.
The cups like the windows were transparent.
The man sported
a tea towel over his forearm
and a thin moustache over his lip.
Three times I went in for a sip of tea
each time he went 'sugar?'
on hearing my request,
looking for the answer like it was of genuine interest.
But now the tea bags are packed
and the sugar-spoken waiter
doesn't cater.
The notice pressed against the glass
simply says thank you
and how sorry they are to go:
a little bit of Deptford
disappearing through the window.

The love between two dogs

I know a dog who's very naughty
he barks when no one's at the door
and sometimes they find things of his
that they shouldn't find on the floor
on the floor
and I love that dog
I adore that dog
I want to have more than a dialogue
with that dog
he's a boy that boy
I'm a boy as well
love don't depend on gender
love depends on what you smell like

Rex

They have a dog
it is lost
they are offering a reward
it is more than the dog cost
they can afford it.
They are second-century Romans
they want their dog back
it is part of their home,
it is a black one
it eats sticks.
It is six.
They have described it on a notice,
it is nailed to a tree,
the notice, not the dog hopefully.

Leaving the festival

Found – slightly breathing
late night on the track
a seemingly knocked over dog.
We tip our torch into its traumatised eye
and see the light reflected lifeless back.
One of our worried number
hurries to bring help back from the gate
while we remaining three kneel around in reverence,
fearing an imminent severance
from life's
security.
Suddenly the heaped hound
hears some sound
other than our tender mumblings
and ears become unslack
it bolts up
and belts out into the black
barking its blinking head off.

Guy

After attempting to bake a cabinet
he got
a more permanent underground plot
and some well-fitting furniture of his own.
Now the proprietors
of one of his many manikins
want some money.
Give them a penny
and they think you're asking for it,
even though they asked for it first.
After agreeing on a fee of fifteen pence
I make a little joke about fawking out
which fails to go off.
I would have paid more
if they'd paid a little more attention to period detail.
People did have feet in the seventeenth century you know.

Bonfire feelings

in their mutual breath
in their startling desire
in their tongue twisting antics
in their surge of unresisting
in their franticness for frolic
in their urge for middle-merging
in their utterings of fever
in their butter-fingered fiddle with the fastenings
the priest reminds the newly weds
that a symbolic kiss is all that is required

Pat at the pool table

Pat's about to pot the yellow,
her arm is to and froing
a bit like somebody bowing
a cello.
She's going
out with a fellow
who likes to think
he's got her in his pocket
but his pocket's got a hole in
and she does all the sewing.

Malcolm

Miserable Malcolm from Morcambe
had Rottweilers but would not walk 'em.
They were stuck in all day
but no muck would they lay
because Malcambe had managed to cork 'em.

The PhanTom

Slightly before three o'clock
she knew there to be someone at the door
in spite of no knock
or any other ordinary indication.
Letting in the night
and a child whom she knew to be an apparition,
she turned back into the light
hoping to find only things of substance
but the ghostly presence persisted.
Shivering in an armchair,
a small boy sat
and something told her that
it was her son
as yet unconceived.
'And what do you think you're playing at?'
She enquired with quite considerable courage.

The trouble with the tampao

In the Portuguese hotel
the plug is not snug
so I lag it
with a bit of a plastic bag.
This works well as a solution
but there is a snag;
after my ablution
when I pull out the plug
the lagging gets dragged into the plumbing
and it won't let out the water.
When I go down to get the porter
to come up and have a look
I have trouble finding something suitable
in my phrase book.

The manœuvre

Doing the tidying in my bedroom
I'm having a job to tell:
shall I lob on that cassette again
or should I let my little radio
tell me something new,
the agreeably familiar
or the challenge of the uncharted?
I decide to put on both
and do a bit of hoovering as well.

Popping out for a paper

I won't be going in my car
because it isn't very far
and because I haven't got a car
I'm not stopping out,
I'm just popping out
for a paper,
shopping for a reality shaper.

McKenna

Me and McKenna started the Duff Gang together
which only kids with duffle coats could join
and only if they were our duffle coats
and only if they had us inside them.

Once I went round his house and we had chips in the
garden. When I got home I told my Mum and she said it
was common, which apparently was not a good thing to be.
McKenna was the first best fighter in our class but was
generally restrained with his power. At my birthday party,
when another boy pointed out that he had on the same
jumper as he wore to school, McKenna did not punch his
face in until after the party, out of respect for my mother.
Instead of a bike like most of us, McKenna had a trolley,
made from old planks and an old pram; he also had a stone
for playing football. McKenna introduced me to another
world and a number of new words and concepts, like 'lodger'
– someone who lived in his house and helped pay the rent –
and 'prostitute'.

Anyway, one day Miss told us that she had an exciting
new project for the summer term. It was to make a model
medieval jousting fair, which made me and McKenna excited
because it was vaguely connected with war, although Miss
explained that the matchboxes McKenna used as soldiers
could do with some paint as well as imagination to help the
rest of us recognise what they were supposed to be. The
completed fair was a rare achievement and children were
brought in from other classes, other schools and other
planets, to stare and to share in the magnificence. But one

day me and McKenna and a few possible new Duff Gang recruits crept past the dinner ladies and into the classroom, where we stood for a while in silence at the altar of our creation.

And then the devastation began. Tents were flicked over at first, then flattened with fists, as was the plasticine queen which Miss herself had made, and whose intricacy of detail all had admired. The surface of the little lake was covered in spit and the heads were bitten off all the little knights in armour, except McKenna's, because they didn't have any. When it was over we knew we had gone beyond the bounds of decency and we shrank back to the playground with our shame, agreeing to say nothing to the rest of the class and to share their horror on the return from playtime.

When Miss came into the classroom it was I who was first to tell her the horrible news.

'They must be found and punished,' she cried.

'Yes Miss,' I said, standing up in outrage. 'Look, did anybody see anything?' I asked the class in a threatening voice.

There was no reply, only McKenna behind me, mumbling that we must own up. Luckily Miss was crying so much she hadn't heard. I turned and made desperate begging emotions that he should reconsider, indicating how I had got myself in even deeper by standing up in outrage and asking if anybody in the room had seen anything, in a threatening voice. But McKenna was decided and he stood up and let it be known that he was guilty. 'And WHO McKenna and WHO?!' she went; she meant 'And who else?' but was too distraught to make proper sense. In slow succession the hands of the other culprits were raised, finally and just about visibly joined by my own. She bolted out of her chair and explained that she had never hit a child but was really going to hurt us for doing this. Surprised and confused that she was not singling me out in any way for my despicable deception, I was relieved to be treated as a common offender, in spite of the threatened severity.

After the hurting, at home time I rushed up to my friend and went 'And WHO McKenna and WHO,' just like Miss had and he looked at me with eyes filled with despising, in spite of my skilful impersonation, and I went home fearing that I was heading for expulsion from the Duff Gang and separation from my best and only friend.

In her office the next afternoon the headmistress soberly asked us the reason for our unwarranted vandalism, having been too busy to deal with the matter in the morning. I explained that it had all occurred when I had slipped and fallen during a game of tag with these other children. I said that the fall had made me have a nasty turn, which in turn had made spit come out of my mouth and go into the little lake by mistake. We were given the doubt's benefit and on our way out McKenna did a bit of growling and scowling but there was to be no emotional disembowelling and, going home, I sang, knowing that I was still eligible for the doings of the Duff Gang, although McKenna

was to increase my weekly subscription
from sixpence a week to a tenner.

Overwriting the Bank of England

The Queen wears glasses
but not on any of them Bank of England banknotes.
She wears many a gem
but not the sparkling jewels
of her glasses
and there must be some occasions
when she's wondering where they've gone
but we can help the Queen
by taking pen to paper
and carefully putting them on.

Spring

sitting tight
white
upright
and unopened
they are a bit like candles
and they make things look holier
these April flowers of the Magnolia

Summer

the fan heater gathers dust
the dusk
gathers later
than in winter
and the elastic gathers my underpants
much the same all year round

Italian holiday snap

Amidst the once pompous pillars
of the derelict Pompeii
feeling the urge to emerge in Roman style
from my companion's photography,
I fashion my tee-shirt into a toga top
while a crop of handy laurel leaves
provide the appropriate hat.
Somewhere in the middle of 'the shoot'
and somewhere in the middle distance
another tourist who has taken an interest in my suit
makes to take a photo of her own.
Beckoning her nearer
to make her picture clearer
I tell her that it's OK
and it's twenty thousand lire.

Autumn

Beside his newly creosoted fence
in neatly folded shirt sleeves
the old gardener vigorously takes his rake
to an overcoat of leaves.
Pausing at a sudden startling pain
caused by an ongoing trouble with the heart
he gets a strong sense
of impending departure
but being a decent fellow
and a tidy chap
before taking the final nap
in a heap of recent rakings
he takes himself indoors
and kisses the missis on the head
then pops back out to put his tools in the toolshed,
thinking that he never did find out what it was
that made Autumn
smell like Autumn
or who it was
who had his pruning shears.

Sumo

It's one of the world's more enigmatic sports
the haircuts are unusual
so are the shorts,
they like their grub and they like a little ruck
they're a little bit like Friar Tuck
but with different haircuts.

Snakes and sheds

The shadow that my shed sheds
I call a sheddow,
a snake does not make much of a shadow
and it doesn't make ANY sheddow
but it can shed its skin though,
unlike a shed.

Street poets

They have my respect,
the genuine men and women of the bottle,
those on the streets
in a constant state of inebriation
locked in their uncommon sense,
when the Martians land
and others are standing round in shock
it is THEY who will extend a hand
and ask for twenty pence.

A Martian tries to buy a drink

This Martian walks into a pub looking like a cross between a plate of hover food and a pair of oven-ready spectacles and asks for a pint of lager top. The barmaid in turn requests proof of age at which the Martian time warps everything forward a quarter of a century and says, 'There, I must be old enough now,' and the barmaid says, 'I'm sorry luv but it's well after time!'

A fisher of words

legs dangle
at an angle
on the slow-wetted harbourside
where I netted the tide
well
just a tiny trickle
of the plop glop slack slop
slip back slap
and tickle

A poem with a pong

This poem is not just to be read quietly
and it isn't just for telling,
it is also for smelling
it is to be sniffed at.
Get a whiff of this,
let your nose kiss the rhyme with unreason
and the next time you blow your nostrils out
your hanky will be all panky
with poetry.

A Bradford curry house

It was a flurry of a curry house.

The lighting was fluorescent and as startling as the smell,
the waiters had white jackets on
and other clothes as well.

Cutlery was by request
for anybody new,
we made asbestos finger jokes
and ate our vindaloo.
It was when I was a student
and it added to the spice
my mum thought it imprudent
but she couldn't fault the price
down The Paradise
in Bradford
up in Yorkshire.

A bloke once sat beside me
and said, 'is it any good?'
He told me he could eat a horse
and probably he would.
I pretended not to hear him
but he kept on being rude
and when he blew his nose on my chapatti
I said 'excuse me, that's my food, mate.'

Relaxing with taxidermy

When their chihuahua got stuffed
they were really chuffed,
no need to feed her
or walkies on a lead her
no more poop to scoop
and doesn't she look smashing on the mantelpiece?
She'll always look at the camera now.
I don't know why we bothered having her alive at all.

Masher

Our dog is no potato
but we still call him spud
he comes out of our patch of garden
by which I mean some mud.
And we wash him and we scrub him
but we don't put him in oil
or baking foil,
we don't put him on to boil
or into soil
because it wouldn't help him grow.
Our dog is no potato.

A spelling of spuds

S – Seldom buried with their glasses.
P – Pebbles that are edible.
U – Underground and roundish
and larger than the reddish
radish,
they are found in rows
but not like those in the cinema.
D – Dug not dog.
S – Severely disappointing as pets
but you don't have to legislate
against pit bull potatoes.

The difference between truth and adequacy

Our Nature of Scientific Activity tutor explained
that with scientific theories
near is
sometimes close enough.
He gave the example of a law
of which science had been sure,
which had been obeyed
unquestioningly since it was made
but which was later discovered to ignore
certain variables;
sometimes what is seen as objective fact
is in fact only a rough guide,
which does the job of ordering
rather than describing reality.
Applying this idea
to what is printed here
adequacy might say
'it's there in black and white,'
whereas I think the truth would rather cite
two shades of grey
of which one's extremely light.

The difference between dogs and sheds

It's not a very good idea to give a dog
a coat
of creosote.

A short address at the comedy college

I hope
you will beware of putting comedy
under the microscope.
To dissect it
first you must kill it,
you must lose the thrill, chill it.
I don't wish my fish
to be a fillet.
Would you beach a whale
merely for teaching porpoises?
I don't want to appear
on a graph
and I don't want to dread
what comes after
the laughter's dead
and that's it, I said.
And as I was leaving the class
I fell on my arse.

Old pals

I was sat unhappily in a chair
on a television programme where
the director made a request
of the celebrity comedy guest;
not to say 'arse' on the air
as it was too dirty
for six-thirty
although it seemed the Pakistani joke
and the ones about 'the wife' were O.K.
Immediately after the show
the comedian added life to a publicity photo
by affectionately grabbing me around the neck.
Maybe I didn't want to betray
his trusting playfulness,
because I disregarded my earlier disgust
and joined in like I'd just had a fantastic time.

Allez

In a park in Calais
a stray dog barks at a Briton on a bench
who is looking up the French
for go away.

French letters – English words

I'd like to commission a poem about condoms she said.
I'll see what I can come up with I jested
and I considered the phrase 'electronically tested'
and imagined the poor little things
shot through with voltage and pain
and thought of starting a campaign
to stop it
and I thought about the campaign
to tell penis-users they might cop it
without one, a condom not a penis that is.
Protection and collection
in those little rubber teats
is something that can save your life
and also save your sheets.

The common poetry

A person waiting to see a show I was doing at the Edinburgh
Festival was handed a leaflet and told that there was another
poetry show he might like to see. I was told that he then
walked off, saying: 'I thought this was a comedy show.
Poetry! Stuff that for a game of soldiers.'

Now what does that phrase mean, stuff that for a game of
soldiers? Is it stuff that for a game of soldiers as in being
above playing with little plastic men, or is it soldiers in the
sense of real soldiers and not wanting to risk getting your
head blown off?

It's neither one of these.

It is both;

it's a compound image,

it is heightened language,

it is poetry.

So ironically the man in the queue was actually using poetry
to say that poetry wasn't for him. What he was possibly
referring to was a certain kind of poetry, currency of a certain
intellectual few, but this is not the only poetic form, as the
man himself had demonstrated. There is a common poetry
which certain poets are committed to enriching, stocking its
pool with ever more dazzling word fish. The common poetry
abounds; rhyming slang, bingo calls, the names given to race-
horses, which are incidentally considerably more imaginative
than those given to dogs.

The common poetry is involved in the re-definition of
language: 'wicked' no longer means merely 'vicious', but also
viciously good. An extension of function, a playing around
with meaning and if you want to play further, instead of

describing something as 'really wicked', you might say it is 'really wicker basket'!

A lick of paint, another instance of the common poetry. I paraphrased this as 'the tongue of the paintbrush giving something drab a dab new sheen'. Three months' work. My earliest memory of the common poetry is a phrase my mother used; she spoke of 'giving birth to the evergreen oyster', when she spat out a big lump of phlegm. I couldn't understand the phrase's relation to the subject, but still it worked for me; it seemed utterly appropriate, transcending mere meaning. Poetry provides more than just a label; evergreen oyster was more than a description, it was an evocation, of what I was wiping from my spectacles.

Easter Eggley

The donkey ride
the road of palms
the garden path
the open arms,
the kiss
the cross
the thorny crown,
the shaking dice
the taking down.
The tomb
the stone
the gathering moss,
the nights without
the dental floss.
The coming out
the new belief
the doubting Tom,
the broken teeth,
the raising up
the making plain:
'Dad, I'm not going back down there again.'

Cause to quibble

In the Cinema Sybil
fancied something to nibble
but the man holding the sweet tray
sold nothing but scribble.

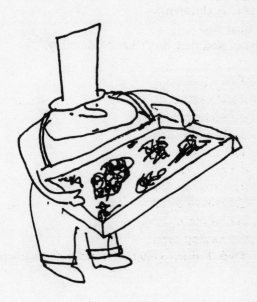

His poems are his children

At night they keep their father from sleep
but then he doesn't want them to sit quietly on the page
and he hopes they will challenge authority.
He hopes he will not be possessive.
He wants to let them live independently
but this will be difficult,
they are his children,
he is their dad
and he is glad they don't have a mummy.

Children's show time-to-go poem

We hope that our piece of theatre
was better than robbers and cops,
we hope you take something away with you and
we hope it's not one of our props.

John put upon

Although John was sat next to me,
when it came to showing sharpness of mind
he seemed to be a long way behind.
When Miss asked the class a question
how frequently my hand would go shooting up
which made John feel uncomfortable
especially if I knocked him in the teeth.

Colette upset

If you ever let
the talented Colette
know that her picture was good
she would always say,
'Mm . . . I like yours too,'
even if it was totally useless (like John's).
But one day
this appreciation of the efforts of others diminished
when in order not to waste paper
Miss distributed for completion
certain partially finished pictures
kept over from a previous class
and Colette didn't like the way
that Miss was trying to work us
and she tipped over the paintbrush pot
and sent the lot
rushing in a slush
over the beginnings of colour
in someone else's circus.
I was quite happy with mine though
it had some animals by the river bank
to which I decided to add a tank and some explosions.

The parade of not-forgetting

In the hotel – very early
the telephone:
'do you have a car in the courtyard
at the hotel front sir?'
'I have no car.'
'Thank you sir.'
I return to a sleep broken hours later
by marching arches, drums and xylophones.
Up at my window the shock
of many blocks of passing uniform.
I remember it is Remembrance Sunday.
Then I recognise the overnight appearance
of two enormous cannons in an otherwise
empty hotel courtyard. I realise
why they asked about my imaginary car.
Some time after breakfast in the public sitting area
I overhear a conversation about white poppies.
'What are they?'
'You know – peace poppies – I think they
should have them on a different day.'
'Mmm – give the cowards yellow ones I say.'
Popping out for a paper I pass
a pair of the parade's participants,
cadets of some sort
carrying what look like real rifles.
But they are only kids, I say,
privately getting all stroppy.
Look – I don't care what colour the poppies are,
just leave the guns out of it,

nobody's going to forget about guns today.
(Especially if they had their car towed away from the hotel
  courtyard.)

The Christmas bonus

To bring in a bit of extra cash before Christmas
my dad answered an advert about going door to door
selling bin-liners which incorporated a king-size picture of
    Santa.
Whether they were for the kiddies' presents
or for the Christmas rubbish I'm not sure
but whatever it was they were for
he didn't want everybody gaping at his business
so after draping a batch of the bags over his arm
he folded his raincoat on top
explaining to me that this made him look respectable.
He then left the home
and dispatched himself into the world of commerce
and I imagined potential customers
witnessing the pulling away of the raincoat like a magician's
    cloth
and although he only sold a couple of units in as many
    hours,
he was always prepared for showers
and all the rest of that year
every time we put the rubbish out
it felt a bit like Christmas.

Neck

We used to have a teacher in our school whom we called
  Neck.
We called him Neck because he had such a long neck.
He also had big sprigs of hair
which came sprouting out of his nose,
but we weren't interested in those.
We were too keen on his neck,
we'd never seen such a neck,
it was a heck of a neck.

Top of the choppers

Grandad's got new dentures
it's great to see him grin,
he got them in a jumble sale
and now he's got them in
his pocket.

Grandma's footsteps

Just because she's got a walking frame
it doesn't mean she's a victim,
she hangs her budgie on the front,
he's nameless
and she nicked 'im.

The gift

A gaggle of schoolboys
noisily join her in the lift;
one of them belches,
all of them giggle.
How pathetic she thinks,
what a shameful show
and she lets them know
by voluntarily belching like a water buffalo.

Borderline decision

Walking around Berwick on Tweed
I bought a Guardian to read,
I had a long train journey ahead
and further into my tread
encountering another paper shop
I decided to stop
and get an Independent in on top.
Not wanting the shopkeeper to feel
I was attempting to steal the first paper
I saw two possible strategies open to me,
one was to state that it was already my property
by standing in the doorway
and calling down to him at the counter,
or more simply I could stuff it down the back of my
trousers,
which is what I did
and I was then able to uninhibitedly
make my purchase in the normal manner.

The crest of a waving

I'm going away on the railway
and I shall be going straight through,
others will change on the journey
I wonder what they will change into.

There's something that's ever so special
about being out on the rails,
going clickety-clack on the back of the track
until something mechanical fails.

Generally though it's fantastic
just buying a ticket feels good;
if you want you can pay with your plastic
but they won't accept pieces of wood.
Would that they would.

Stationary folk on the platform
wave at their friends as they go
but they think that it's weird if you're waving
if you're not somebody they know though.

But once you get out at the station
attitudes rapidly change
and the wave of an absolute stranger
is no longer thought to be strange,
there's a couple curved in an allotment
alloting some time to be tall
waving away in their rhubarb
like they're not rheumatic at all.

But last night I dreamt that the railway
was out of the public domain
and none of the public had any desire
to wave at the privatised train.
Not even the Railway Children.

The Cumbrian cutting

In the hotel a broken pane
and the pain of a broken skin
as the glass went in
and my finger began to leak
and to make a little lake
like I hadn't come to look at.
There's nicer prices to pay
for a piece of poetry tinder;
my main memory of Windermere
was merely of a winder.

Not my cup of coffee

On the train I have asked for coffee
but my travelling companion has mistakenly got me a large
  tea
(because this is what I have usually).
I am not annoyed,
we cannot avoid such errors.
I tell my friend it's O.K.
but before going back to the buffet
I ask the people sat opposite
if any of them would like the unwanted beverage
for half the recommended price.

Tales from the tent

Yawning, he lent forward in his awning
and unzipped the morning.
Unfortunately he unzipped tomorrow morning by mistake.
Fortunately he wasn't awake.

Friendship in the Mendip Hills

Even though I went
to the trouble of putting up your tent
for you,
it was fine
that you spent
all of your time
in mine.

The creeping sleeping bag

One day when I slept on a slope
my sleeping bag crept downhill
and I invented the phrase 'it crope'.

The power of rhyme

I realised the power of rhyme within my first hour on the
infant school playground. 'Do you like jelly?' I was asked.
'No,' I replied . . . 'I'll punch you in the belly!' I was
playfully advised. Do you like blancmange? I'll tread on your
foot – so much less effective.

Talking about my feelings
ain't my cup of tea

Please don't do the third degree
about the two of us
or the one of me
'cos I ain't one for talking about my feelings.
I just get these mental blocks
if it's insecurity the box it's in is ever so secure
with a very well-kept key;
talking about my feelings ain't my cup of tea.
Once when I had a nasty gash in my knee
and the doctor questioned me
about how I'd come to hurt myself
I was only too glad to be forthcoming
but enquiries about how I hurt myself
in the sense of self pretence and things like that
they make me want to flee:
talking about my feelings ain't my cuppa.
Anyway who wants to know
that someone thinks existence stinks
or that every day spent on this planet
is one less day to go.
I'm not referring to me though,
it's just an example.
It's no big deal.
I keep my cards so near my chest
even I can't see the way I feel.
I used to be closer to my emotions
or maybe they were close to me.
In the past I've been very open

the last time was when I was twenty-three
months.
They say bashing pillows is beneficial
and it helps to hug a tree.
They say problems shared are problems halved
but they don't say it to me
because revealing how I'm feeling it isn't my Darjeeling.

J for jealous

I was in short trousers and I was in love with Jane but was unable to say so. I had been given no schooling about expressing this emotion, and felt I couldn't talk about love anyway, because, being as I was the seventh best fighter in the class, it seemed best not to mention love. So I would content myself with constantly kicking her under the desk. This gained me her attention, if not her affection. At least the words were similar.

And then Wojtek came along. He was brought to the front to sit next to Jane so Miss could keep her eye upon him. And Wojtek began to pay his own attentions, saying that she had beautiful hair and neat work, which she seemed to prefer to being kicked. Soon I became obsessed with their exchanges and I'd make fun of her, saying, 'You love him, don't you?' hoping that by expressing my greatest fear it would never happen and I tried to kick her in a nicer way but it was no good now and as their bond grew, so did my jealousy and I didn't know what it was. J was for jelly, not jealousy and jealousy at that time was worse for me than it is now. Now I know that, however horrible it is, eventually it will end, but I didn't know that then. All I knew about this sickness was that it seemed terminal and there was no support system available.

And then one day I saw them kissing in the playground and I could bear it no more, I had to speak my pain and I told Miss and they both got the cane because Miss said kissing was dirty and then I was caned for telling on them because Miss said that telling tales was pathetic. And when school was over Jane ran out after me and banged me in the teeth and said how she hated me and so relieved was I at having her attention again, I wept, and out came a blathering that I was glad she hated me because I had loved her all along. And she banged me in the teeth again and she said if I loved her I wouldn't have kicked her under the desk and if I loved her I'd be glad that somebody else was making her happy. But I wasn't the smallest bit glad, so I don't suppose it was love after all.

Meditation on 'The Raising of the Cross' by Rembrandt

Looking up, the Lord looks like he would read the note
nailed above his head.
He has a special relationship with the word.
Maybe in the life to come his Dad will tell him what it said.
In the darkness the Lord is light
but as those executioners might tell you
not when combined with the weight of this damned wood.
The spade is stood at rest
having played its part in the passion
here where beards are in fashion.
In the middle, the riddle of Rembrandt
assisting with the deed.
Perhaps he feels the need to declare his responsibility,
his sins are also being died for.
The horse of course is not guilty
in spite of the role of its rider, the commander,
who, like the viewer, is from the wrong period.
In the background one of the thieves prepares
for his bit part departure.
History will give him a mention
although it will not recall his name.
And on the other side what could be an apostle
requesting mercy
unsure that his boss'll
really rise
again.

Outsider art

As a bit of a break for Albert
from the hospital of the mind
I accompanied him to the park for a picnic
and a bit of crayoning enjoyment;
using just the one crayon
he liked to attend to a piece of paper
and meticulously obliterate the surface area.
Some time into the process
a couple who shared Albert's middle age
came sneaking a fascinated peek
over the shoulder of what they took to be
an amateur landscape artist
but found his interpretation of reality
just a little too modern.

Otto Dix art attack

I heard them on Radio Three,
the Critical Faculty,
piling it on about his great grotesquery
but expressing their dismay
at how greatness had gone away
by the end
and I wanted to defend him,
I wanted to say
that I knew something they didn't about Otto:
what you do best
won't be what you do last
was his motto.
The critics had a go at Otto Dix
for not being any good when he was seventy-six,
or however old he was,
but after those past decades of exhausting brilliance,
in his retirement,
why couldn't they allow a chap
to paint for pleasure
and to be crap.

My brother's advice

The morning I started out for infant school
my older brother told me to remember
that girls never prosper
I don't know where he got this motto
nor did I understand its meaning
but because he was my example
I repeated the words to everyone I met
and did not get a girl friend until I was twenty-seven.

My father's admonishment

When my father condemned me
for behaviour he announced as abnormal
I countered with a condemnation
of his holding of normality in such esteem
explaining that what was deemed to be normal
wasn't necessarily sane.
I said that although it was considered normal
to anaesthetise yourself stupid in front of the television
the sanity of such an exercise was questionable
and my father asked me how sane I thought it was
to walk around the house continuously belching.

Greed

Once when I wanted all my sister's sweets
I pretended to be a hungry dog
and each time she dropped one on the floor
I amused her with my comical scavenging
and when all her sweets had gone
I stopped and got on with my own
taking no interest in the hungry dog
that looked very much like my sister.

The daily bread

On his first day Bert
wore a skirt
to the building site
which surprisingly
his workmates chose to ignore.
I suppose it was because
he was so different from them anyway
what with his nose on the top of his head
and his bread that said Saturday's score.

Poem without a heart

He's into mirrors
he's into sound
he's into crowds
and crawling around.

He's into wool
he's into string,
he's into polystyrene,
he's into everything.

He's into sticks
he's into stones
he's into questions
and ansafones.

He's into eating
he's into air
he's into cats
and he's into care.

Trains in India

Indian railway transportation
has no buffet facility
and so travelling on the railway
when you pull into a station
local people bring you buffet stuff on their own.
Getting off briefly in such a situation
I go for a coconut
and the vendor agrees
to open one for me
if I tender three rupees.
As he does so I consider the unliklihood
of British Rail introducing buffet bar bartering
or machetes.

Fresh in Edinburgh

During my first festival wash for a year
looking at the lather appear
I think gosh this soap's good gear
and then remember how much softer
the water is up here
although something beside the sink
makes me think
that the stink of dried facecloths
is more universal.

The flannel

I believe this society to be
deeply keen to enforce
distinctions of gender
fearful of a course
of cheerful androgyny.
It starts with the naming of the progeny.
Apart from a few anomalous instances
there are separate names for either sex:
'If it's a boy we'll call him Tex
and if it's a girl, Octavia.'
And the con
goes on,
from codes of dress and behaviour
down to the smallest print of existence.
I was struck by all this
after a lucky purchase in a high-street chemist;
asking to be supplied with a flannel
I was politely directed to a little sub-section entitled
MEN'S FACECLOTHS.

Declaring Martian Law

One morning John fashioned the beginnings of a poem which went in the following fashion:

A DOG CALLED THE FISH

There was an old Man called Mrs Mish
Whose dog was called
The fish.

That was enough for one morning's grafting. John dropped his pen and propped his spectacles further up his nose. He felt reasonably satisfied with the crafting but wished the character he'd invented had shown something more in the way of the emotional life.

Popping into the newsagent on his way to the gaff of his favourite caff, he purchased 'his usual' as the man behind the counter referred to that morning's copy of John's usual. John warmed to such recognition of his own existence; innocent little attentions like that could make him quite tearful, but not this morning, as he was too busy contemplating the man in his poem who didn't show any emotion. Arriving at the caff he quickly scanned the few customers therein for anyone who might have a sudden psychotic outburst. There was no such person apart from himself and John sat down at his ease and at his usual table.

'The usual, John?' asked Harry who was the gaffer in the caff's gaff.

'Yes, it's the same old usual John,' John joked, not an important joke but enough to get a laugh out of Harry, because more important than the joke was a warmth of intention, to which Harry had readily warmed. John liked everything about Harry's caff except for the lack of a customer's lavatory and the occasional psychotic element in the clientèle.

Harry returned with not only John's weak tea but with a newspaper as well. 'Paper, John?' said Harry. 'No, I'm a flesh and bone John,' John replied.

Harry subconsciously noted that this joke was inferior to its predecessor and offered his customer the newspaper. Rather than say I've already got one and yours is more like the Beano, John readily accepted and proceeded to browse through the pages. Harry's paper might not have much in the way of arts coverage, thought John, but it had an earthy well-used feel to it; the various eyes that had scanned it that morning had invested it with a significance not shared by his own unopened usual. Like the Mona Lisa, it was not what it was that made it but how much it had been looked at; the imbibed vibe of the many viewers, thought John.

'Anything to eat?' said Harry.

'Sorry,' said John. 'I was miles away.'

'I wish I was,' said Harry.

John smiled at Harry's rejoinder and ordered his meal. Passing through the sports pages he saw a lot of rings around things in the horse racing section. 'WHAT ARE THESE MARKS HERE?' John suddenly shouted into the kitchen. 'HARRY, WHAT ARE THESE MARKS? HARRY, LOOK; THESE MARKS, WHAT ARE THEY? THESE MARKS, HARRY. HARRY!!?'

Harry reappeared, slightly alarmed.

'Are you all right, John?' he asked.

'I'm fine,' said John, drawing Harry's attention to the marks. 'But what about these marks? They've damaged your paper.'

'It's O.K., John.'

'Thanks, Harry.'

Harry returned to the kitchen and John began to scan the lists of strange names which people had given the racehorses in the hope of invoking success. He came across one which he found most striking: 'A Dog Called The Fish'. At that moment Harry appeared with John's usual meal.

'What a very strange coincidence,' said John.

'What's that?' asked Harry, interested, but also interested in arranging John's cutlery.

'Well, just as I was reading the paper you brought my meal.'

'Just a coincidence,' said Harry, casually.

John smiled and began his meal. He actually preferred it much cooler than it was served but usually started eating immediately as he didn't want Harry to think him odd or ungrateful. As he munched away, his thoughts turned to betting shops. He wasn't particularly keen on them but he rather enjoyed being in the presence of freely available betting shop biros: cheaply made, without embellishment, things which didn't need to entice the consumer into purchase, outsider products in the capitalist economy.

During these deliberations, John's mate Tony made his entrance. 'Amico, brother,' said Tony, freezing in the doorway with one hand held up like someone half held at gunpoint. 'Amico, brother,' said John, entering into the little performance. 'Sit yourself down – no, not on the chair – in my meal.'

Tony sat on the chair and addressed his companion.

'What have you been up to then; more of that blessèd poetry, no doubt?'

'Yes and Pat's gone.'

'What do you mean, gone, John?'

'Gone to live in Greater Manchester with Boris.'

'You never loved her anyway.'

'I did love her, Tony.'

'You didn't.'

'I did.'

'Did you, oh. Written any poems about her going yet?'

'No. But have a look at this one I wrote this morning. What do you reckon?'

'. . . Mm . . . rubbish, quite funny though.'

'Yes, I think maybe it's a bit short.'

'The short ones are always the best.'

'But you said it was rubbish.'

'But at least it's short rubbish, John.'

'Mm, anyway what are you up to?'

'I'm going off to stay at me mam's for the weekend.'

'From what you've said she sounds like a right old eccentric.'

'Looks like one as well, John; I think you'd like her though. Tag along if you want. You'd love her cooking.'

'No – I'm going up to Greater Manchester to sort out this Boris nonsense.'

'Please yourself, you ungrateful old duffer.'

Tony asked John what time his train was going. John consulted his watch, looked surprised, and called out, 'Harry, I've got to go, I'll leave you some money on the table.' He put a piece of paper with 'some money' written on it on the table and tipped the remainder of his meal into one of his two duffle bags. Then Harry appeared at the counter still wishing he was miles away and asking if he could come too. John said that he could and Harry followed him out of the caff flapping his hand and making his fingers click together in the way people do sometimes to demonstrate their pleasure.

As the train moved out of the station a man and woman standing in the gangway next to John and Harry were arguing about where to sit.

'I want to sit looking at my luggage.'

'But it's safer to sit facing the other way.'

'Look, I want to see my luggage in the vestibule.'

'Well, have you a mirror?'

'Yes, but it's packed in my luggage.'

'Well, let's get it out.'

'But it's a big mirror all packed up with brown paper and string.'

'Excuse me,' John interrupted, 'but did you mention brown paper?'

'Sorry?'

'Brown paper?'

'What of it?'

'Well, yesterday I wrote a poem containing a reference to a brown paper parcel.'

'Fascinating,' said the arguee John had addressed, dismissively returning to the previous conflict.

'It's not like getting a little mirror out of your toilet bag, you know.'

'Excuse me,' said John.

'WHAT?!'

'The same poem had a reference to a flannel in it and you just mentioned a toilet bag. What were you going to say next?'

'WHAT?!!?!'

'What were you going to say in your argument? Maybe it was something else in my poem?'

'Do you think you could mind your own business?'

'Come on, darling, I'm not staying here,' said the arguee, disappearing up the gangway. 'It's been a dog called the fish of a day today,' she said, but John didn't hear.

Harry had been oblivious to the whole incident, and was looking about himself in true fascination at the new environment.

'Makes a change from the caff, eh, Harry?' said John. 'Let me get YOU a cup of tea for a change.'

'No,' Harry answered. 'I'm going to the buffet myself, to explore the world of the train.'

Harry returned, reporting that the buffet was shut. 'It's shut, but those sliding doors – wow. Imagine *those* in the caff!' John was envious of Harry's first-time excitement about train life, seeing someone else enjoying themselves like this highlighted his own over-familiarity with the environment. But this was no reason to be resentful. Indeed, he should encourage Harry's marvelling.

'Those doors would be fantastic in the caff, Harry.'

'No – they'd be useless,' said Harry. 'Far too narrow. I'm going to see what the toilets are like now.'

'It's a shame you haven't got one of *those* in the caff, Harry.' Some time later, Harry made a more successful excursion to the buffet and returned with the teas.

'Here, guess who I've just seen at the buffet?'

'The buffet steward?'

'Correct.'

'Here, Harry, do you want a game of something?'

'How do you play it?'

'I think of something and you ask questions to find out what it is.'

'All right, is it a dog?'

'Yes – your turn.'

'O.K. Is it another dog?'

'Yes!'

'Was it really a dog?'

'Was yours?'

'No.'

'Mine was!'

'What was it called?'

'The Flannel.'

'I wouldn't have got that. I know another game. You've got a minute to talk about a subject without coughing. You go first: I want you to talk for one minute about why there are no toilets in your caff.'

'Oh look, we're here.'

'Where?'

'I don't know, we're somewhere else now. Listen John, I don't want to talk about the caff. I'm trying to get away from it, it's my livelihood and it's dear to me. It's not perfect, but it's not naff, and it's dear to me, but for now I don't want it near to me. Is that clear to you?'

'Sorry, Harry. Excuse me, Sir, do you mind not smoking? This is a non-smoking compartment,' said John to a nearby passenger, who was actually just transferring his cigarettes from one pocket to another.

'Oh great,' said Harry, 'a tunnel.' In the tunnel, John suddenly went into a reverie and recollected a song he'd composed for Sherlock Holmes and his faithful companion in his children's theatre days:

I am Sherlock Holmes
and I am Doctor Watson
my bow tie is yellow
and my bow tie's got spots on
my name isn't Jackson
and my name isn't Jones
no I am Doctor Watson
and I am Sherlock Holmes

Meanwhile, Harry was considering a Chinese customer of his. She worked in the Chinese takeaway across the road. He was feeling proud that someone in the business would want to patronise his caff. He remembered her complimenting him only recently on a plate of scampi he'd dished up. Fancy that, thought Harry. She must be able to get food cheap over where she works but she comes to *me*. And I don't even do Chinese food and yet she comes to me. He focussed in more closely on the scampi incident. He remembered how respectful were her compliments. No, there was more than respect, he had seen it at the time but hadn't realised. It was something else; they came out of the tunnel and he knew he must return. It was love.

'John, I've got to get off,' said Harry. 'I have unfinished business at the caff.'

'You don't have to go yet; the train's doing a hundred miles an hour. Let's have a game of something else. How about hangman?' said John, taking a noose out of the duffle bag, which didn't have any dinner in it. 'One person pretends this is something other than what it is and the other person has to guess what. Look – what's this?'

'Someone driving a car?'

'What make, though?'

'Erm – a Rover?'

'No, a Mitooki – made the name up. Your go.'

'O.K. What's this?'

'A loophole in the law?'

'Yes, your go.'

'O.K. What's this?'

'A dog?'

'Yes, but what breed?'

'A Mitooki?'

'Yes, your go again.'

Harry got off and his place opposite John was taken by a man using calipers to get himself along. After he had settled in the man took some papers out of his briefcase and spread them over into John's bit. John continued writing poetry on his noose until he was interrupted by the sound of a muffled mobile phone and when the man took it out of the case and took the call in a very loud voice John decided he should say something.

'Please, if you're going to use this as an office, could you try and be aware that there's someone sharing your desk who's got work to do as well?'

John had once been to a comedy show where a man in a wheelchair had done an open mike spot and had started telling racist jokes. The offended audience had been slightly hesitant in demonstrating their displeasure because of his disability but when he kept on at it they finally told him to go and he said, 'That's it, heckle a cripple.'

John sensed that disability wouldn't be made the issue here and he was right. The man told John he was doing the wrong thing with his noose writing poetry on it and, relieved, John picked up the noose and said, 'O.K. What's this?'

'A Mitooki,' said the man.

'Yes,' said John, 'your go.'

When the phone tootled again the man curtly told the caller he was busy playing hangman and couldn't talk. The phone didn't come out of the case again and John suspected the man might have turned his tootler off so they wouldn't be further disturbed, which John thought was very nice of him. A little later, his newly found companion put on his walkman and turned it up to a volume loud enough to be heard in the next compartment and John assumed they were having a break in the game.

The man got off at the next station stop, after which John nodded off and dreamt that he was in the city centre of Rome some two thousand years earlier. It was night time and he approached a row of citizens under the Olympic torch-like street lighting, glad of his opportunity to use his elementary Latin. Why hadn't his teacher mentioned the possibility of time travel when she had explained why the language was worth learning? Engaging the citizens in conversation John was informed that this was a bus stop, that they were waiting for the IV night bus and that if he valued his life he should get to the back of the queue. When the transport arrived, referring to John's spectacles, the conductor said, 'What are you playing at with that stupid jewelry on your face? You tourists make me sick,' and he ran him through with his broadsword. As John lay writhing on the pavement a small chariot came by driven by a Samaritan. Unfortunately it was a bad Samaritan. Fortunately, some Christians came by next and they transported him to the nearest apothecary.

Apparently the apothecary could work wonders, if you had the money, and John enquired about the possibility of credit.

'I'll pay you back as soon as I'm fit enough to work.'

'What work's that, then?' enquired the apothecary.

'Er – I'm a soothsayer.'

'Prove it.'

'All right. One day they will have machines that will take pictures through your skin so you can study bones and the internal organs.'

'Mm – X rays, another soothsayer told me about them. O.K., this is my assistant, Patricius, she'll sort you out. If anyone needs me, I'll be out in the shed playing with my chariot set.'

'So what's he like to work for?' said John, after the apothecary had gone.

'Fortunately he prefers boys to women, so I don't get any harassment in the workplace.'

Patricius put a dab of ointment on the injury and John felt a lot better and went out into the street saying sooths so as to pay the bill.

'One day they will have night buses without horses, and

chariots with wings and chariots that will visit the stars.' To make the job more interesting, he embellished a little: 'And one day they will have chariots that you can fold up and put in your pocket. There will be technological marvels,' he went on, 'and they will discover the beginnings of the universe; yet in terms of human interaction and a sense of community they will be worse off than mice.'

Patricius applauded from the audience and John told her he'd fallen head over heels in love.

'Head over heels, huh? You'd better be careful you don't open that wound,' said Patricius. And from somewhere an unfamiliar voice said something like 'MANCHESTER PICCADILLY. ALL CHANGE PLEASE. THIS TRAIN TERMINATES HERE.'

John remembered why he was making this journey. He was here to visit the girl friend who had recently terminated their relationship and he was making a last ditch effort to get it unterminated. He called her from the station and arranged a meeting location.

After ordering a weak tea in the designated caff he plonked himself down and began chattily enough but soon it all turned unpleasant.

'Anyway, what about you, Pat, have you done any new paintings? No? I wonder why that is. Too busy with Boris, eh? Is that one of his jumpers? . . . Even if it is a present it's a bit insensitive wearing it, don't you think? It's a horrible jumper. Is he horrible? I think he is. I think I'd like to give him a present. Let's see what Father Christmas has got in

his bag. Here, a little noose, and I've got some dinner loose
in the other one; he can have that as well. I'm sorry, Patricia
– we don't need this, do we? I've just come up here to give
you the chance to come back if you want to. Look, you go
and explain to old Bozzer, I'll go and book us a hotel and we
can take all your stuff back in the morning except the
jumper. What do you say?'

John hadn't really expected it to go too well and as he
made his way back to the station he was glad he had taken
the precaution of booking a seat on the train home.

Harry was to do rather better. On his return he visited the
woman in the Chinese takeaway. That evening he took her to
the Albert Hall with a couple of tickets he'd obtained from a
tout who used the caff. It was a great success even though
he'd been mistaken in thinking that Sumo was essentially
Chinese.

Back in Greater Manchester, John thought that showing
Pat his new poem had not been the best beginning to their
meeting. But he had asked her about her work afterwards
and she hadn't done any anyway.

He'd guessed it would hurt if it didn't work out but you
can't really judge the depth of a hole until you're falling
down it, can you? He'd not thought she would come back,
but the possibility that she might had given him a bit more
time before he'd started falling. You fell in love and then
you fell down the hole. He took out his pen and made a note
of the line on his usual. Hey, maybe I'm still asleep! He shut
his eyes and opened them up again but it was as he

suspected. He wasn't asleep. He wanted his usual world, not this world of misery. What time was it? Five thirty-two. The pubs would be open.

He found one.

'Yes, mate?'

'I'll have a weak tea, please.'

'No tea; weak, strong or medium – and we don't do coffee either.'

'Where's that accent from; it's not from Manchester, is it?'

'No.'

'Anyway, sorry, I meant a half of weak lager. I was miles away.'

'I wish I were 'n' all.'

'Sorry? You wish you were . . . ?'

'Wish you weren't here, mate. No. I wish I was miles away 'n' all. It's no great shakes, bar work.'

'Maybe you should work in a cocktail bar instead.'

'Why?'

'Great shakes, you know.'

'Mm – anything else?'

'Yes, I'm saying the wrong things, but my intention is not to be antagonistic and maybe you think I'm a bit of an idiot. Well, that's what I think as well.'

'Nothing else, then?'

At that moment, nothing was exactly what John wanted, but instead he bought a packet of peanuts. He sat down with the peanuts, the beer and the sense of loss and consumed all three quietly in a corner. This was no good. He needed to keep in contact with the world. He suddenly upped and returned to the unoccupied barman and asked if he could read him a poem.

'Poetry. Not too keen on poetry. I'll give it a go, though, go on.'

John dug out from one of his duffle bags a poem and a drawing from the previous day:

THE WASH

Beside the English Channel
in a village on the coast
a certain Englishman'll
get a flannel in the post.

And he will not know who sent it
and he will not know what for
and although he's washed already
he will wash himself once more.

And he'll wonder why
whoever sent the flannel through the post
never sent the towel
that he needed the most.

And when the washing's over
the Englishman will sigh
and he'll pick his little doggie up
and use it to get dry.

'What do you reckon then?'

'Rubbish. Quite funny, but it's rubbish.'

'Do you think the dog should be called "The Fish"?'

'Mm . . . that'd be all right – good name for a dog, that.'

'But if the dog were called "The Fish", you wouldn't get so much comedy out of the man drying himself on it because fishes don't mind water and by implication nor would the dog, so it wouldn't have that element of misfortune that people tend to laugh at.'

'Mmm . . . why don't you have the dog biting the bloke and then the bloke changes its name to Piranha?'

The barman went to serve another customer and, aware that more human communication was what he needed, John went and made use of the telephone.

'Hello Tone, what are you up to . . . ? Look, is it all right if I come along? I could do with some fresh country air . . . I don't mind how many she smokes a day . . . mashed potatoes – love 'em. Look, are you sure it'll be O.K. for me to stay? If not, say . . . right, I'm on my way. . . . The station buffet. Great. Cheers, mate. Yeah. Amico.'

Outside, it had begun to rain and John looked up and allowed it to pepper his face and pain, taking a breath before taking the direction of the station where he would obtain the departure time of the next train to his newly acquired destination.

There were forty minutes of waiting before his connection and for the waiting time he was grateful, comforted in the knowledge that this was time with a purpose. Putting his small bags on an unnecessary platform trolley, he pushed out to the appropriate platform's end. Here, beyond the buffers and buffets and almost out of earshot of the station announcements, he stretched out among the concrete slopes that marked out the margins of the station. He thought how silly that more people didn't move out of the shadows and share in the opportunity of sunshine. Only the trainspotters took the chance. Others would make fun of them, thinking their own pursuits of gathering fame, money and children to be superior; whereas in the final oblivion where everything is

redundant, what more appropriate activity than
trainspotting? With such thoughts, John lay down among
their number and slipped into a slumber. Here among the
deviants he felt able to be deviant himself. It was hardly
devastatingly aberrant behaviour to lie out on a platform and
rest in the sun, but it was still unacceptable to the majority.

> John had a dream about Pat
> and they seemed to have forgotten
> that their relationship was rotten
> and they were walking up an avenue
> hand in hand
> with a brand new understanding . . .

John was awoken by a trainspotter kicking him and saying,
'Get up off the floor, you weirdo.' He looked at his watch
and saw that his train was about to pull in.

'Thanks,' said John, trying to defuse the aggression.
'Thanks for waking me, my train's about to pull in.'

On the journey down from Manchester, John gazed into
the passing picturesquery and pieced together some of the
past with Pat. Their first meeting over the snooker table,
their second under the mistletoe; the passion that kiss had
led to and the feeling that they were two Roman gods
literally making love for the good of all man and womankind.

'ALL TICKETS PLEASE.'

'Oooooooh – that was a bit loud, wasn't it?'

'I'm sorry, sir, but I need to alert the whole
compartment.'

'But there's only me here.'

'Could I see your ticket, please, sir? . . . Thank you, you haven't left your bags in the vestibule, have you, sir?'

'No.'

'Where are they?'

'There they are on the rack.'

'A shame you're not too, isn't it, sir?'

'What?'

'It's a shame you're not being tortured on the rack, then you wouldn't have to worry about me doing my job, would you?'

As the guard handed back the ticket he purposefully dug his nail into John's hand, then moved down the carriage, shouting 'ALL TICKETS PLEASE' to no one. When he had gone, John decided to take advantage of being alone in the compartment and lifted up his tee-shirt and tenderly squeezed out a blackhead, wishing he could get rid of the muck that infiltrated his relationships with such ease. He decided to try and shift his thoughts elsewhere and for the rest of the journey immersed himself in a book full of blocks of letters which contained hidden words which you put a line through with your biro when you found one.

Looking up and catching himself and his book in the window's reflection. John reflected upon how a good book could transport you in times of need, just like a good train, but not a *goods* train, unless you were a stowaway or whatever such people are called. At the end of the journey, John sought out the station buffet. He now had a bit of a wait and bit of a weight in the sense of your troubles weighing you down, but at least he had his book.

'A weak tea, please, luv,' said John. He didn't really feel comfortable saying 'luv', but he wanted to come over as normal. However the man behind the counter didn't take much to John's mode of address.

For a moment, John thought he'd lost one of his duffle bags, but then he remembered he'd pushed it down his trousers so he wouldn't seem like a weirdo with two duffle bags. He sat down and, poring over his puzzle book, he felt a bit like Sherlock Holmes again. Dear, oh dear, oh dear, oh deerstalker, he said to himself.

When Tony arrived, John had a very welcome laugh when his friend said, 'Are you just pleased to see me, or is that a duffle bag down your trousers?' Tone said they'd need a cab as the last bus had gone some years ago.

The man who opened the door at Tony's mum's wore a hair net and a pair of horn-rimmed glasses which John found intriguing.

'Yes, the lenses got scratched, so I decided to remove them.'

'But what good are they now, if they don't help you see?'

'No good at all. You two go in, we're having mashed potatoes. I'll just go and get some spuds out of the potato shed.'

In the kitchen, John asked, 'Is that your dad, Tone? I got the impression that your mum lived on her own.'

'Look, John, my mum's dead, and now she's gone Dad likes us kids to think of *him* as our mother. She'd prefer it if you say "Mrs McKenna", even though she's really a man.'

'I was telling John how much you enjoy potatoes, Mum.'

'Oh yes; I don't like blight in the blighters, but that's pretty normal, isn't it? Tony, show him up to Dad's old room; I've made up the bed for him. You can put his bags up there. Duffle bags, aren't they, John? Very nice.'

As John sat up in the bedroom, he thought that this was crazy and it was just what he needed to diminish the feeling of finishing with Patricia. Then he found himself thinking about how much she would have loved meeting Mrs McKenna and he knew that Pat wasn't going to be that easily forgat.

The meal was a simple one of mashed potato and nothing else. Afterwards, Mrs McKenna had a bit of work for the boys, assisting her sticking in polaroid photographs of individual potatoes taken after they had been cleaned and before they had been mashed.

Before John went up to bed, Mrs McKenna explained that her husband had always preferred candle light and had never fixed the electricity up there and she hoped he wouldn't mind. John said that he loved candle light, although once installed in the bed he doubted if her husband had also preferred sleeping bags to sleeping between sheets. He began making random candle shadows on the ceiling, to see what might arise. His favourite was a Roman soldier, the fingers of one hand being that skirt thing which they wear. His least favourite was a giraffe.

That night, John had a number of dreams, the first of which included a nest of ants which were really giraffes and the last one saw him back in Rome in the caff under Patricius's home.

'A weak tea, please, Harrius. What are you up to, Pat?'

'It's a postcard to my brother – he's a centurion in Britannia. Do you want to read it?'

'No, you read it.'

'All right. "My dear Lucius, I'm sat in the caff recovering from the moneylender above me having another party last night. Honestly, I lay in bed thinking they were having a gladiatorial contest up there. I confronted him about it this morning. I said, 'What did you think you were playing at?' and he told me they were having a gladiatorial contest up there. My gods, that island certainly doesn't sound like the best reason for having an Empire, but, by Jupiter, I bet you're glad you're in a town with some decent baths! Well, I must finish now, as you know, writing on these tablets wears your arm out in no time." '

'And who's the other one to?'

'Oh . . . that's to my sister, it's a bit personal.'

'Come on, Pat, let's have a look.'

'No, don't, John, it's private.'

'Come on, I thought you were all for all property being public, come on, let's have a look . . .'

'Hey, your sister's changed her name to Boris: "My dear beautiful Boris." '

'Don't, John.'

'Who's beautiful Boris, then? Someone who needs his legs breaking by the sounds of it.'

'He's in a wheelchair already, John.'

'And is his wheelchair some sort of motorbike, by any chance?' John enquired.

John awoke to hear a revving sound outside. He got up and leaned out to find Tony on an old BSA Bantam 175.

'Where did that come from, Tone?'

'The shed. My mum bought it ages ago.'

'What, your dead mum or your living mum? Ha ha.'

'His living mum,' said Mrs McKenna, appearing from the entrance of the shed with a bulging hessian sack.

'Sorry; I'm sorry,' said John, feeling sorry for being the fool that he was. Often he would tell himself to remember to think before opening his mouth, but he kept on forgetting.

'It's O.K., son, I know it takes a bit of getting used to, the man being the mum.'

'Yes, and it's a bit strange having nothing but mashed potatoes for dinner,' quipped John, invigorated by such ready forgiveness.

'Don't start mocking the food I give you, lad, if you don't mind. That I don't like.'

'Sorry; I'm sorry.'

'She's winding you up, John,' said Tony, as his mum took the sack indoors. 'Come on, let's go for a ride.'

'Hold on, I haven't had a wash yet – and who cares, who cares?' he said, hurrying downstairs in his pyjamas and slipping into his shoes and out into the shimmering blueness of an everlasting summer.

'Have a bone dome, John,' said Tony, handing his friend the spare crash helmet. 'Make yourself at home. There's a stone circle in the next valley, I think you'll like it.'

'Don't you want any breakfast?' called out Mrs McKenna, visible at the kitchen window, where she was scrubbing up potatoes.

'We'll have it for lunch, Mum,' called back Tony, turning up the throttle and slipping them across the gravel and out into a summer that stretched back in John's mind to him sitting two-up on the back of Tony's childhood trolley twenty-odd years previous. He gripped more tightly on to his friend's jacket and maybe not all the tears in his eyes were caused by the wind. There was a spluttering and a jolting and the bike came to a standstill.

They took turns in pushing the bike back to the house, where Mrs McKenna told them not to worry about the trip not working out as there was plenty to occupy them in the digging up potatoes department. So they dag and they dag all the day and at sunset they put their tools away, put the spuds into sacks, stretched their backs and came indoors to relax.

'What have you been up to, Mum?'

'Oh, I've just been talking to my potatoes. No, seriously, I've been doing some accounts. Not quite as much fun, as you can imagine.'

'Are you feeling a bit better then, John? Tony told me that you're nursing a bit of a knock from a woman friend, is that so? Yes, well, you know the best thing for it?'

'Mashed potato?'

'No – creative accounting.'

After tea and two and three quarter hours of creative accountancy, Mrs McKenna announced that it might be time for Tony to take John to visit the stone rectangle of the village pub.

'So what's up with your friend, then, Tony?' said the Welsh barmaid, who remembered Tony from a previous visit.

'He's a poet.'

'Quite a problem, then! The weight of the tragic muse, is it?' she said in John's direction.

'This is Miranda,' said Tony.

'Maybe if you shared your muse you might feel a bit less tragic – we could do with a bit of colourful language in here,' said Miranda.

'Go on, John, do one of your poems – but don't do the one about the flannels.'

'Why not?'

'Wet, is it?' enquired Miranda.

John found himself warming to the situation and to Miranda and in the course of their conversation and her candour he discovered that he was in love. She called the bar room to order and introduced poetry's protagonist for the evening. John began the recital, which was well received by the regulars, although the couple from South London found it an unwelcome intrusion. John was inspired by Miranda's laugh and he was glad to be the creator of the poetry which inspired it. He did do the flannel poem, and his companion's advice proved to have been well informed.

'A wet flannel? A wet blanket more like!' challenged the male member of the cynical London couple, at which Miranda tipped the contents of an ash tray into the hood of his duffle coat and John did Hilaire Belloc's 'Miranda' poem in her honour. By the end of the evening, John was very jolly, but when it was time to go and he asked her about having sex, he was told that she'd already had enough fun for one night.

'So you only wanted me for my poetry then?'

'No, I wanted to flirt with you and you wanted to flirt with me. I certainly didn't want to hurt you but I did it for itself, not for what might come after.'

As John and Tony made their way back to Mrs McKenna's house, John was distinctly back in dumpsville and hardly touched his share of the mashed potato supper that had been left out for them.

The following night, after work, John and Tony went down the pub again and on arrival they discovered that it was Miranda's evening off, at which John felt disappointed and relieved at the same time, but not as relieved as the South Londoners were that he wasn't doing another poetry recital. This time, being as it was their last night, Mrs McKenna came too.

The regulars made quite a thing of her visit, although she explained on first arriving in the village they had been very suspicious of Martians. 'Oh yes, it took them a while getting used to the Mrs McKenna business, but once they realised I could put away the mashed potato with the best of them I think they realised I was human enough.'

'But don't you miss the old planet?' enquired John.

'I've never seen it, son, but I'd like Tony to take a look at the place some day. You'll do that for me, won't you, Tony?'

'Sure thing, Mam.'

That night, after handing John his economy-size magic carpet, which was actually a face flannel, Tony laid down his own and sat in position. John did the same and as they whizzed through space Tony explained that Mars was much the same as earth except that the people were green, as was the brown paper.

As soon as they hit the Martian atmosphere, Tony went all green.

'That's how it works,' said Tone, 'Martians only look Martian on Mars.'

'Fascinating,' said John.

As they zoomed into the Martian caff a dog ran out from behind the counter and started barking.

'Here. Fish, good dog,' said the white-jacketed one behind the counter.

'Did you hear that, Tone? Excuse me, mate, is your dog called Fish?'

'No, mate, I'm just feeding him fish. That's why I was saying, here, fish.'

'Yes, but you're changing the inflection now . . .'

'Just relax, John, remember others have problems too.'

'Hare Krishna, Tone; sorry, mate, I think I'm going to tell everyone in the caff a few jokes to cheer us all up.'

'Great idea John, although I don't know how that South London couple will appreciate it.'

116

John realised that his friend was joking and, after doing a joke of his own, he was about to do a second, when one of the Martians got up and said it was her turn. John didn't get to tell another joke until everyone else in the caff had told a joke, including the dog.

'Everyone's a performer here, John. Same as on earth, really, only here everyone gets paid for it.'

'No alienated wage labour then or people begging on the streets?'

'No, John, and no business except show business and the business of improving communication between Martians to take us closer to the stars.'

'Sounds brilliant.'

'Yes, but the biros here are useless.'

At that moment, Patricius, the apothecary's assistant, walked in, but before she could tell her joke, John was awoken by Mrs McKenna calling up the stairs telling him it was time to start digging up potatoes.

That evening, as the boys were finishing off the photo albums and the accounts, the phone rang and Mrs McKenna informed John: 'There's a woman on the phone for you, young man. I asked her who it was and she says to tell you it's someone who's changed her mind.'

In considerable anticipation, John picked up the phone. 'Pat . . .'

'John – it's Miranda,' said the phone.

'Pat the dog, someone. Sorry, Miranda, the dog's a bit depressed here and I was just telling someone to give it some attention,' said John, speedily inventing a brilliant lie which he would later make her laugh about. John and Miranda would see each other again and then again and it would go so well for a while and then it wouldn't go so well and then it would stop going altogether. Again.

I won't go into the rise and decline of this little empire, except to say that John became very possessive and irrational, which culminated in his suspecting that Miranda was secretly having an affair with Sherlock Holmes.

The day after their relationship finished, John had invited Harry and Ho Li round to his place for a meal to celebrate their engagement. John had purchased the ingredients for a curry for four, but now only three would be eating. He began with the onions, peeling off the outer skin, which was brittle and tended to break at the circumference. He divided the bulk on the breadboard and his blade was wet with onion milk. He cupped up the chopped pieces in his palms, hoisted them over to the awaiting pan and dropped them into the heated oil. This moment, the first sizzling, was usually one of life's little happinesses. But not today. Today, it joined the drab drizzle of life without love. He wondered if he would ever experience a clear day again. Would he ever again feel nice simply browning the onions and boiling the rice? People knocked the word 'nice' but today it would do him just nicely.

As the preparations progressed, the phone rang. 'Hello,' said the phone, 'Is that the bloke who went to sleep on Manchester Piccadilly station a couple of years ago with two duffle bags on a platform trolley?'

'Possibly.'

'And someone kicked you and woke you up? And you thanked them for waking you because your train was coming?'

'Probably.'

'Well, I've regretted it ever since. I found you really attractive, but had some ridiculous block about expressing my emotions and it came out all wrong.'

'Yes, I remember that and I remember that I was attracted to you as well. How did you get my number?'

'Getting numbers I'm good at, I'm a trainspotter.'

'Listen, if I tell you my address, would you come and join me and a couple of friends for dinner?'

Unfortunately, the phone had only rung in John's imagination.

The curry went down well with his guests, if a little slowly, owing to the vast amount of chilli powder he'd tipped in in his absent-minded musing.

'Just because it's vegetarian doesn't mean it can't be a real man's meal,' John explained. Ho Li didn't know what he was talking about, but generally found his quirkiness refreshing and both she and Harry were particularly impressed with the microwaved hot flannels.

At the end of the evening, their host suggested they finish things with a bang. He said there was a sky rocket he'd been keeping for a special occasion since the previous bonfire night. At this, Ho Li began to weep and said there had been too many fireworks in Tiananmen Square and if it was the Chinese who discovered gunpowder, they had done the world a terrible disservice. Harry put his arm around her and John agreed it was terrible, but they should still let off the rocket as a symbol of hope. Ho Li agreed and they went out into John's patch of garden and in a reverential quiet he put a match to the rocket, which flew out of the milk bottle and hit Harry in the gullet.

Harry received more shock than injury from the incident and he would be back at work the following morning with nothing worse than a small fabric plaster and the mishap had given Ho Li the release of laughter from her vantage point in the confines of the shed with John's little dog.

The next morning, John went down the caff. He noticed that a nearby customer was eating egg foo yung and chips. Egg foo yung and chips? thought John. Ridiculous. Looking around the caff he noticed that everyone was eating egg foo yung and chips. Then the caff door opened and in came Miranda. Then the toilet door opened and in came Sherlock Holmes.

'Harry, you've got a toilet!' said John.

'Now, how did that get there?' said Harry.

'It's a mystery,' said Sherlock Holmes. 'There I was on the trail of that Baskervilles hound and suddenly I'm here. It's a different kettle of dog altogether.' Holmes and Miranda ordered egg foo yung without chips and sat down with John, who went straight into his declaration of need:

I need you like a kitchen needs a cook
like a copper needs a crook
like a look-a-like needs somebody to look like.
I need you like a postman needs an address
I need you to say yes, I need you by express
I need you like I don't need this distress.

'It would seem that he needs you,' said Holmes. 'But perhaps you need him rather less. I propose, sir, that your love is an imposter which makes of Miranda a thing to cling to and that is why you have already lost her.'

'Is this true?' asked John, and Miranda clarified the situation.

'I don't need you to talk for me, Holmes, nor do I *want* you to. No, John, his analysis is not true. But it is adequate.'

That night, John went into the bathroom to make a model tent out of his radiator-stiffened facecloth for the benefit of some plastic boy scouts who found life in his trouser pocket uncomfortable. As he picked up the tent-to-be, a moth flicked out from underneath and he gave it a quick telling-off for trying to scoff his facecloth and then got on with erecting the little awning, using for tent poles two biros which he pushed into some plasticine. John considered his creation and squashed it flat in a fit of anger at the discrepancy between the cheerful scene he had created and his own miserable situation.

John's dog then suddenly came charging in, demanding an explanation of this hideous destruction and John asked the meaning of the word 'hideous', to buy himself the time to concoct an innocent story. He then explained that he had lost his balance during a game of tag with himself.

In such a confined space with no one else present, the dog knew this to be nonsense, but was impressed by the use of the imaginative faculty and John was merely cautioned with a bit of growling.

John patted the dog and tried to remember a theory he favoured; he was just a single cell in the multicellular organism of humanity. He ordered himself to remember that his aim was to participate in a global consciousness that would make his own troubles seem microscopic. Then he began to weep. And through his tearful bleariness, it seemed he saw the face of Miranda looking up at him from the flattened facecloth. John picked it up, went over to the sink and stood waiting for it to fill with water, while the dog contendedly chewed away at the plastic boy scouts. John spread the cloth, closed his eyes, and reverently wiped away his crying. When he looked about him again, to his surprise it was morning and he was standing on Manchester Piccadilly Station.

In front of him was the sound of sobbing coming from what looked like a heap of rags. If he couldn't help himself, maybe he could help somebody else.

The heap of rags turned out to be a heap of facecloths. And looking deep into the heap John saw the faces of the trainspotter, Miranda and Patricia, and possibly even Jane, his first love from his primary school days. Putting on his glasses, he found that the incredible sight was the same, only slightly clearer.

'All right, so you've found me,' said the facecloths. 'Now it's your turn to hide.'

'What do you mean?'

'Once you've found what you're looking for, that isn't the beginning, that's the end.'

'Look, I'm a bit confused,' said John. 'I think I need to go home.'

Needing to immerse himself in the usual world, he had bought another of those books full of word puzzles and working away with his biro he gradually and gratefully came down to earth. Getting off the train, he immediately made for his usual caff, where for the first time he was glad to see the absence of a customer's lavatory.

'A cup of the usual, please, Harry.'

'Hello, Tone. How have you been going on?'

'My mum's gone, John.'

'Gone?'

'You know, John – she's left us and her remains are installed within the earth.'

'So what's the good news?'

'She's left me the motorbike.'

'How do you feel?'

'It'll never get through the M.O.T. I'm all right, John, and yourself?'

'Well, something a bit unnerving has happened to me, actually, Tone. First, a strange dog starts talking in my house and then I'm mysteriously transported to Greater Manchester, where I undergo some kind of emotional catharsis with a heap of facecloths. It's weird, isn't it?'

'It is, John, but the *fact* of existence is weirder than any of its manifestations, isn't it? My dad was my mum and my mum was a Martian, but what's weirder than that is that she's not here any more. She's left *you* something as well, John.'

'What is it?'

'See if you can guess.'

'A Mitooki?'

'No.'

'A Pakooki?'

'No.'

'A Babooki?'

'Yep, and there's something else.'

'What's that, Tone?' and Tony told him.

'Potaters! I might have guessed!'

'No, John, not potaters, pesetas.'

'Oh yeah, how many?'

'A sackful.'

'Do you fancy a trip to Spain then, Tone?'

'A small sackful.'

'Bournemouth?'

'A SMALL sackful.'

'Another weak tea, then, Tone. Two weak teas, please, Harry. One weak tea deserves another, eh Tone?'

'Mm.'

That night, John found himself standing in a crowd on a hot afternoon, in a scene he recognised from the Bible. People around him were throwing down palm leaves in anticipation of a figure on a donkey a short distance off. At first, he felt rather uncomfortable not really knowing anybody, but as the central figure drew closer John recognised him not only as the Lord but also as the barman he'd chatted with in Manchester. The crowd broke ranks and the Lord came unto John.

'I thought it was a bit strange, that pub being called the Lord's Inn,' said John. 'If I'd been Sherlock Holmes, I'd have realised: the beard, the halo, the sense of bar-work not being your true vocation.'

'It gives you a chance to meet people, though, and get an idea of whose salvation you'll be dying for,' said the Lord. 'By the way, I hope you don't mind, but I've called my dog The Fish.'

'How come they don't mention your dog in the Bible?'

'Ask me another.'

'How does it feel to be a celebrity?'

'Ask me that next Friday.'

The Lord moved on and, finding that his pockets were empty, John found a market place elsewhere in the city where he gave a rendition of 'Jerusalem' by William Blake, which soon earned him the price of a magic facecloth, which suddenly whisked him up into the shimmering blueness, where he felt like an American superhero, but one who wore his glasses outside of his secret identity.

Until, that is, he was knocked out of the sky by a bombardment of King Edward potatoes. John awoke the next morning remembering the spuddified trip to his friend's parental home. What would he have done without all that? He began to contemplate Tony's loyalty over the years.

A tear appeared in his eyeball and John felt an urge to action. After enclosing his body in his jacket he went out of the door and down to the flower sender's shop where he made an unusual purchase of four bunches of irises which he directed to his companion's address along with the following message:

> So many have loved me
> and left
> but for all their leaving
> I have never been bereft of love
> because there has always been
> this quiet love of ours
> and here are some flowers.

The following morning, John received a note from Tony, saying that he preferred the one about the fish.